Self-Esteem

A Step-by-step Guide To Discovering Your Inner Artist Making The Most Of Your Skills, And Realizing Your Full Creative Potential

(Learn How To Conquer Your Fears, Boost Your Confidence, And Accept Who You Really Are)

Wilburn Ferguson

TABLE OF CONTENT

Get Yourself Confidence!...1

Maintaining A Constructive Dialogue With Oneself On A Day-To-Day Basis................................7

Making Headway In The Business World..........11

Increasing One's Level Of Self-Assurance Is Associated With An Increase In Overall Happiness...20

How To Set A Goal Or Resolve A Problem.........24

Honor Your Own Sense Of Worth And Dignity. 38

Do You Consider Yourself To Be A Pessimist? 47

Altering Feelings Via Changes In Behavior.......57

What Is Self Confidence?..63

How To Make Yourself The Centre Of Attention In Your Own Life...70

Overcoming Unproductive And Negative Thoughts 86

Both Strengths And Challenges Characterise Highly Sensitive Introverts. 97

The Numerous Advantages Of Increasing One's Self-Confidence..119

How To Figure Out What It Is That Drives You
.... 126
Honor Your Own Sense Of Worth And Dignity.
.... 145

Get Yourself Confidence!

Purchasing confidence is yet another tried-and-true method of boosting one's level of self-assurance. It is not possible to purchase confidence in the form of a pill or capsule, since this is not what I mean. There is a good chance that I am not referring to the practise of acquiring spirit in the form of some Iron Man–like contraption that envelops one in an incredible veneer of self-confidence. They subscribe to the outmoded notion that a person's appearance may determine his or her success. A significant number of individuals also persist in the mistaken belief that one must look as if they already had one million dollars in order to achieve their financial goals.

In other words, the exterior aspects of your look are the ones that are responsible for reorganising the aspects of your life that take place on the inside. This puts it completely in the other direction, as we shall go through later. In actuality, the opposite is true. If you want to have confidence, you have to cultivate it from the inside out before you can show it to other people. You have to begin at the core of who you are as an individual and then work your way outward. Building on top of a strong base like this is how it's done. To the contrary, if you construct your identity based on how other people see you—for example, via the use of toys, gadgets, and other baubles that you purchase—then you are dependent on your exterior shell to alter your interior self. The big benefit of purchasing your confidence is, first and foremost, that it is a simple and fast process. You may buy yourself some respect by purchasing a variety of trinkets and electronic devices if you have a credit card or a profession that allows you to make purchases. Now, bear in mind that you are not earning anyone's respect by doing so. You are deceiving yourself if you believe you can purchase respect. You are just giving other people's responses more positive connotations than they really deserve.

You are essentially capitalising on the mental sloth of other individuals by doing what you are doing. They start with a sign, and then they imbue it with a variety of different meanings. For instance, if you drove into the parking lot in a brand-new Ferrari, people would first glance at your vehicle, then look at you, and make a variety of snap judgements about the link between the two of you. People are quick to leap to the conclusion that you are a winner, that you have made it, that you are the top dog, and that you are a leader when they see you driving a vehicle that costs several hundred thousand dollars since it is quite unusual for someone to drive a car worth that much money.

It is possible, as you can well guess, that all that happened was that you borrowed the Ferrari of a buddy. It's possible that you're a technician working on that Ferrari and you're merely putting it through its paces by driving it around town. On the other hand, individuals are psychologically slothful. They accept a sign at face value and instantly put all kinds of meaning onto it, often drawing from their lack of self-confidence. Nevertheless, this method of conveying assurance is both fast and uncomplicated.

Now, there is a significant drawback to using this approach. To begin, there is a monetary investment required. The higher level of self-assurance that you want to convey, the greater the financial investment that will be required. For instance, if you ask your friends from high school over for a drink at your house and they show up at a mansion, the cost of purchasing that mansion is going to be quite a deal more than you first anticipated. Two, you are putting on quite the show here. You are conducting your life in accordance with the expectations of other people. In other words, the fact that people are interpreting meaning into what you are doing is the return that you are looking for. It has nothing to do with what you have created for yourself and by yourself. It is completely unrelated.

You have to put up with appearances even if this is already very difficult for you. You have to realise that people only offer respect reluctantly, and for a lot of individuals, nothing would make them feel better than to watch someone who they consider to be superior to them slip up and collapse. You have to realise that people only give respect reluctantly. This, of course, results in a significant increase in levels of stress.

In addition to this, you have the underlying sensation that you are a liar or an imposter. You have the impression that now that you have acquired the outward manifestations of self-confidence, it is only a matter of time until other people discover the truth about you. The level of tension caused by this is enormous. This may put a significant amount of stress on your nerves. You have brought this upon yourself, unfortunately, when you believe that your trinkets, financial goods, and other outer trappings ultimately determine who you are. If you are unable to keep up with the costs of maintaining appearances, then this is going to be an issue for you. When others start seeing you differently as a result of your change in luck, it may have a negative impact on both your sense of self-respect and your self-confidence.

Maintaining A Constructive Dialogue With Oneself On A Day-To-Day Basis

You should engage in positive self-talk for the duration of the day in order to establish another example of reasoning. You will most likely have built up an example of negative deduction for a long time, and this will set aside effort to survive. To begin with, you should anticipate to rehash positive self-talk around multiple times for the duration of the day. This can be accomplished by rehashing positive proclamations inconspicuously to yourself or out so anyone might hear. You may use positive self-talk to aid you in conquering challenging situations, gaining faith in yourself, helping you to quit habits, recovering quicker from illness, or making improvements to your life as a whole. All of these benefits can be attained by practising positive self-talk. Well-known phrases or statements are some of the elements that may be used into positive internal dialogue.

• I have an interesting test ahead of me – instead of looking at the circumstance in a negative manner and thinking that I have a problem, thinking of it as a test is a significantly more positive way to manage it. This can be used whenever there is a problem that arises in everyday life or when there is some sort of difficulty.

• I enjoy the person that I am – this may be used to boost fearlessness and enhance respect for yourself and the person that you are; equivalent reasons might be "I am the best", "I am a decent individual", or "I have numerous great characteristics."

• I am confident in my ability to do this task - use this affirmation if you are confronted with a particular assignment that you would first question your capacity to complete; alternatively, you may say "I am able to complete this" or "this does not present a challenge for me."

• I am loaded with wellbeing, vitality, and significance – you may use this to boost positive feelings about your wellbeing either after you have been incapacitated or while you are recovering from a disease. • I am loaded with wellbeing, vitality, and significance – I am loaded with all of these things.

• I am content with myself as a person - you may use this to motivate yourself to have wonderful general good thoughts about yourself and the world in which you live.

Making Headway In The Business World

There are some types of businesses, such as networking corporations and brokerage organisations, that have a significant need for the extroverted and talkative characteristics that extroverts possess. The characteristics of introverts, on the other hand, are starting to play a more major role in the market as a result of the advent of the digital era.

People are now able to participate in conversation via the exchange of material, in contrast to the past, when communication was done in a unidirectional fashion and encouraged little to no involvement. This calls for careful consideration as well as a strategy that encourages participation from others. Because of the traits that introverts already possess, it is inevitable for them to achieve success in the field of marketing in the future.

1. Information that is meaningful.

Many companies are moving away from the conventional method of selling face-to-face and towards the practise of marketing online. They not only end up saving a significant amount of money, but they also end up reaching a much larger number of people. On the other hand, this results in congestion on the internet.

There are hundreds to thousands of commercials that try to attract your attention by flashing, popping, glittering, and performing other types of exhibitions. These attract the attention of everyone, similar to way an extrovert does, but they are also simple to ignore, particularly when done so from behind a computer, since individuals have the option to be indifferent and judgemental towards other people and situations. Content is the most important component of what constitutes a successful marketing campaign on a digital platform.

It just so happens that introverts have an advantage in this particular domain. They are able to write extremely insightful and intelligent material that can retain anyone's attention because they listen, observe, and digest information in a way that allows them to do so. The next step is to urge others to participate in the campaign by sharing, like, retweeting, and other similar activities.

2. Communications that go right to the point.

Messages are at the heart of what businesses do. This is always the initial phase in the process, and it is intended to pique the interest of prospective customers. However, as the internet has become more congested, audiences' attention spans have developed to become confined to microseconds. Extroverts often begin conversation by engaging in small chat, and they use the same method when promoting their products or services online. However, the vast majority of individuals want to steer clear of these situations whenever they can, and they are able to do so from the convenience of their own homes. This is something that a lot of introverts can identify to. They are not interested in idle chatter, which is why they get right to the subject at hand. Messages that are direct and get to the point about what the sender wants others to know tend to get a higher grade of attention.

3. Improved quality of relationships.

Introverts, who are the polar opposite of extroverts, are ready to construct "marriages" on the digital platform, while extroverts are focused on securing "dates." This indicates that they are more inclined to participate and reply to any point of view provided by readers after posting a material, in contrast to their rivals, who are often happy with only receiving likes. Introverts are the best people to go to when trying to make connections, whether they take place in real life or online. Connections are more important in today's world than having a large reach, and introverts are the best people to go to when trying to do so.

4. Those Who Are Initiated and Values Cooperative effort.

It's not uncommon to come across things on the internet that convey a sense of individualism in their words. Some marketing initiatives out there put so much emphasis on themselves that they obscure the attention of most people rather than excite them. They do this without realising the consequences of their actions. On the other hand, introverts are firm believers in the merits of working together with others. They understand that the combined efforts of numerous thoughts and players may deliver more moving messages and greater outcomes.

5. A disposition to be open to the contributions of others.

Giving and receiving are essential to the functioning of a balanced online ecology. Sharing significant material that was uploaded by others may help marketers reach a broader audience and build their reputation, provided that they provide all of the relevant information about where the content originated and who owns the rights to it. Introverts, as opposed to extroverts, are more likely to be receptive to this concept, and they could even be the ones to make the first move.

6. Authenticity as well as openness and honesty.

The fact that it is simple to identify falsehoods spread throughout the internet is the key component in the strategy of sowing seeds of uncertainty among internet users. On the other side, introverts are quite straightforward in their communication, and their comments are never sugar-coated or embellished. To put it another way, what you see is exactly what you get. They don't have any need to conceal anything beneath the rock, thus you won't find anything there.

The conduct of business does not necessarily take place face to face. Because of advancements in technology, introverts now have the option of working from the privacy and security of their own homes while yet maintaining the same level of productivity as their extroverted colleagues. Take use of the things you are excellent at and use them to your advantage in order to achieve the goals you have set for yourself, since this is a common piece of advice given by successful individuals. You are not required to constantly act in the same manner as everyone else. Introverts are resourceful individuals who are able to depart from the standard and create their own paths by using tactics that are not often used. The one and only thing you need is to properly equip yourself with information, which you have already accomplished just by reading this book.

Because it is already a part of you, there is no specific component that is required to increase your strength. Your strong, introverted intellect can only reach its full potential if you are aware of its powers and, of course, believe in yourself.

Increasing One's Level Of Self-Assurance Is Associated With An Increase In Overall Happiness.

while a person has a healthy degree of self-confidence, they naturally feel more confident while they are carrying out duties, which eventually leads to a greater success rate; as a result, they are able to feel good about themselves, which ultimately leads to more confidence, which finally leads to more pleasure. Individuals who make their living participating in self-esteem-boosting programmes and courses People who are happier and have more life satisfaction tend to exhibit greater levels of self-confidence, according to several reports.

People who have a higher level of self-confidence have a tendency to take on the world with a greater level of ferocity and conviction. This, in turn, enables them to have a greater sense of connection with their surroundings, and they naturally feel a higher level of contentment and security in their relationships. Naturally, they also have a greater power to influence other people, and they have the abilities to regulate their own behaviours and emotions in a more compelling manner. This is because they are more confident in themselves. Because of this, effective leaders throughout the globe have a tendency to have a greater level of self-confidence, which garners respect from their followers in a natural manner and eventually results in a working atmosphere that is both healthier and more functional. When a person likes themselves and has a healthy regard for themselves, they tend to have a more upbeat and optimistic outlook on life, which is one of the key components of self-confidence.

The notion of what brings about pleasure is one of the least well known topics in the whole universe. When asked about the source of their pleasure, most individuals would respond with one of the following:

Getting a better career, Buying a better automobile, Finding a significant other, Having a kid, Having more money, and Purchasing a nicer home are some goals that people often have.

There is a consistent thread running through all of those responses, and that is the fact that virtually all of them are materialistic. Neither having things nor purchasing things can bring about satisfaction on their own. When a person has too many stuff, it may often lead to misery, which is the reverse consequence of what one would expect from having more possessions. The capacity of a person to comprehend their own internal nature and to maintain a lifestyle that is congruent with that comprehension is the true secret to that person's contentment. If you are able to identify the aspects of your life that are most important to you,

you will be in a better position to formulate a strategy that will lead you to your goals. You need to motivate yourself through building up your sense of self-worth in order to accomplish those goals. A person must have self-confidence in order to recognise what adjustments or compromises they will need to make in order to attain the goals they have set for themselves, which are outlined in the list that was just presented. If a person does not have faith in this, they are likely to have feelings of disorientation, helplessness, and confusion about why life isn't fair and why they are unable to have the things that other people do.

How To Set A Goal Or Resolve A Problem

People often say things like, "I am aware that this is significant to me, but I am just not that motivated." These individuals seldom begin anything new or make any changes because they wait to be motivated before they do so. They seem to believe, for some reason, that the only way they can get closer to anything (or farther away from something) is if they are motivated. Not true!

They somehow have the expectation that inspiration will materialise out of thin air, and that this will enchant them into taking action in the direction of their objective. Do not sit about waiting for motivation to somehow materialise on its own because it does not, and it will not. No matter how long you wait, the motivation bus will never come. You may as well give up.

What comes next is a statement of the utmost significance.

DO NOT wait until you feel motivated or until you get motivated.

If what you want to do is essential to you but you don't feel motivated to work towards it, you should force yourself to complete the task regardless of how you feel about it. Make the conscious choice to carry it out. It is possible that an act of will, discipline, and determination will be required to accomplish this. Yes, it is possible that it will be unpleasant, that it will need a commitment from you, and that you may be required to forego doing something else.

Nevertheless, you carry it through because you are aware of the final result, which is your objective; this is more important than whether or not you are feeling motivated at the time. The majority of individuals make the mistake of concentrating on what they will be required to sacrifice rather than what they will stand to gain in the long run.

Do you really believe that elite swimmers look forward to waking up at 4:30 in the morning on a daily basis to train? They are totally focused on the end result; their objective, rather than resenting the fact that they have to get up early in the morning. That is what propels them on, and it is what serves as their primary source of inspiration.

What is it that you value the most?

Just get things going in the right direction in order to make progress towards a goal that is significant to you. Begin to push that ball of inspiration until it gains its own momentum, which it will, and once it does, it could even be difficult to top. As the well-known slogan for Nike proclaims, 'Just Do It!' Or, to paraphrase a well-known quote often attributed to Johann Wolfgang von Goethe: "Whatever you can do or dream you can, begin it." The phrase "boldness has genius, power, and magic in it"

It's the same as beginning an exercise routine when you haven't done so for a long time, or even ever. It is quite unlikely that you will roll out of bed one morning brimming with inspiration and eager to get started working out.

You may not be in the mood for it, but you force yourself to get moving nevertheless because you know that in the long run, doing so will make you feel better and contribute to your overall health. At first, it will require a significant amount of effort, and you may find that you have to struggle against the little voice in your head that will provide you with a variety of compelling reasons and opportunities to avoid doing it.

This is a really significant point. The more you engage in the activity, the more inspired you will feel! The more that pressure is applied to the ball, the more momentum will be created by the ball itself. It's the same as trying to push a rock up a hill. When you push a rock up one side of a hill, it becomes progressively more difficult to do so as you approach the crest of the hill.

The moment that most people should be making their breakthrough is the one in which they throw in the towel. However, if you push that rock over the edge, it will generate its own momentum, causing it to roll downhill more quickly and for a longer distance as it continues to build up more momentum.

So keep that in mind. It's not always going to be easy to find the motivation to work on the things that are most important to you. Don't sit around and wait for the inspiration to strike you. Make the determination to carry it through anyway, and then get started building momentum. You will soon discover that the momentum will continue even without your participation, and it is possible that it may even pull you along with it.

Having a Poor Opinion of Oneself

A lack of gratitude towards oneself might be the outcome of low self-esteem, which can lead to self-defeating mentalities, mental helplessness, social problems, or dangerous practises. This is a crucial view to have since it provides the desire to embrace the idea that one's self-esteem has to be examined not just as a reason but also as an effect of problem behaviour. For instance, children could have a pessimistic opinion of themselves, which can cause them to feel depressed because of the association it has with the negative image. On the other hand, feeling horrible might be the consequence of being discouraged or not working well, which can lead to a reduction in one's self-esteem.

It is also believed that having a low self-esteem might be a risky element, one that can lead to insanity and even confinement. People who don't trust themselves are unable to cope with the problems of daily life, which in turn hinders their ability to achieve their fullest potential. This might result in a decline in both one's bodily and one's mental well-being. A decline in one's emotional health may be the cause of behaviour that is intended to conceal other problems, such as sadness, unease, or problems with one's food.

People who had healthy levels of self-esteem were able to make more consistent and global internal attributions for positive events than they did for unfavourable conditions, which led to the strengthening of their positive mental self-view. Subjects who had a low level of self-esteem were more likely to attribute negative experiences to consistent and global internal factors, whereas happy events were more likely to be attributed to external factors and luck.

In studies that followed people over time, having a poor self-esteem throughout infancy, pre-adulthood, and early adulthood was shown to be a significant predictor of sadness in later years. When the cumulative stress, social support, and self-esteem were given successively in relapse assessment, only self-esteem exhibited crucial depression of the three factors.

Studies on eating disorders make clear consideration for the key function that self-esteem plays throughout the formative years of education. At this stage of life, behaviour about one's weight, body form, and the act of calculating calories becomes intertwined with one's personality. In young female students and teens, having a poor self-esteem has been identified by researchers as a risk factor that contributes to the development of dietary difficulties.

Individuals with low self-esteem tend to be more wary of the potentially negative outcomes of therapy in situations like these. Because of the significant influence that self-esteem has on an individual's perspective of themselves, several programmes have been developed in which the cultivation of self-esteem serves as the main means of dietary issue prevention. In conclusion, there is a consistent relationship between having high self-esteem and implementing problem behaviour into one's daily life. In addition, there is a considerable amount of circumstantial evidence to suggest that low self-esteem may contribute to the dissolution of assimilation of problem behaviour, while an increase in self-esteem may be able to prevent such disintegration.

Numerous researchers in the field of science have identified self-esteem as a crucial component in the process of preventing unethical behaviour, facilitating recovery from it, and bringing about societal changes, despite the fact that the causes for such practises are varied and difficult to anticipate. It is interesting to note that both low self-esteem as well as high and inflated self-esteem are associated to the improvement of troubling symptoms.

Low self-esteem and a negative attitude may make it difficult to take responsibility and constructive criticism, which can block you from situations and subsequently hinder you from taking on new tasks, which ultimately prevents you from having meaningful interactions throughout your life. It also has the potential to sever important ties. It is possible for us to have low self-esteem for a variety of reasons, each of which may have an effect on our emotions, our thoughts, and our actions, as well as demonstrate how we see and interact with both ourselves and other people. The reasons for this include rejection from people who are important to you, tying your sense of self-worth to outcomes that are beyond your control and that make you feel like a loser if things don't turn out the way you want them to, as well as psychological concerns such as personality disorders and feelings of hopelessness.

My Aim in This

For me, it all began at a time when I had reached the lowest point possible in terms of my self-esteem. I didn't like who I was at all, and while I felt powerless, I wanted to alter that.

I made the decision right then and there that I was going to do all in my power to get those levels as close to the maximum as I possibly could. I was well aware that I have the ability to transform my self-esteem into one of my most valuable assets. And now I am on this never-ending road to wake up liking myself each day and have such a robust feeling of self-assurance in myself and my abilities.

Although there has been progress made in raising awareness of mental health, there is still a long way to go, as the statistics on suicides unfortunately reveal. Problems with one's self-esteem and confidence don't quite rise to the level of a diagnosable mental illness, but they may undoubtedly play a role in the development of conditions such as depression and anxiety. In my life, I've had times that were quite depressing and worried, both of which originated from having a terrible view of myself.

This has to be cut down right now. People have to work to overcome the poor self-esteem views that they have in themselves. In this book, as well as in my other writing, as well as in my videos and podcasts on YouTube, as well as in my coaching and mentoring, I will do all in my power to assist individuals in raising their own levels of self-esteem and confidence.

In the most recent few months, there have been instances when I have surprised even myself with how good I feel about myself at that same moment.

When I am able to go into a room full of people and talk to them in such a composed and self-assured manner, it never ceases to astound me. I have a deep appreciation for who I am and I always have the sensation of being in a happy relationship. I want an extremely high percentage of individuals to agree with you on how they feel about themselves. I also think that if more people had strong self-esteem, the world would be a much more loving place, since the only people who harm other people are the ones who are hurting themselves. My goal is to facilitate a beneficial domino effect in which individuals love themselves, which in turn has a good influence on the lives of others.

I first became interested in personal development because I believed that I needed to improve, but now days I pursue it because I care about myself and love myself enough to want to offer myself the greatest life possible. I do not need anything else, but I like receiving assistance even more.

Honor Your Own Sense Of Worth And Dignity.

It is time to celebrate your self-esteem, and the more you do so, the more optimistic your ideas will become about yourself. It is not a tough procedure to comprehend, and it is not even difficult to carry out. The difficulty is to have persistence since that is how you win at this game. persistence is the key.

Affirmations 2 is a recording by Louise Hay.

Several chapters' worth of coverage was devoted to revisiting Louise Hay and her use of positive affirmations. This point bears repeating since it is fundamental to what it means to persevere. You will notice an instant boost to your confidence after engaging in the practise of positive affirmations; nevertheless, it is imperative that you continue engaging in the practise. Your level of happiness, love, self-confidence, and fulfilment will all increase if you follow this course of action, as will your sense of self-worth.

Ensure that you speak the affirmations aloud on a regular basis and at numerous points throughout the day. "Every day, in every way possible, I am getting better and better." It is necessary for you to either consciously experience these affirmations by listening to them or subtly experiencing them when you are sleeping or meditating. Therefore, allow these affirmations to take hold inside of you. Let them develop to their full potential. Continued effort.Continued effort.Continued effort.

By Substituting One Negative Thought About Yourself With One Positive Thought About Yourself

As was shown before, ideas have a material existence. Thoughts have the power to bring forth physical manifestations. It is possible for thoughts to become manifest directly from the energy that they are composed of. The world is shaped by our thoughts. As a result of this, you have the ability to immediately boost your self-esteem by changing one of your negative self-thoughts into one of your positive self-thoughts.

Continue in this manner. You will gradually replace any negative self-thoughts with more positive ones as you continue to work on this. Affirmations allow you to take control of your future and make changes there without affecting the past. Nevertheless, the current moment is where you should focus most of your energy to improve your sense of self-worth. RIGHT NOW. Don't put it off till the next day. Begin now to rid your mind of negative ideas and replace them with good ones.

Establish Objectives

If you accomplish what you set out to do or at least put in a good faith attempt to do so, goal setting may be an effective tool for improving your sense of self-worth. Do not use the process of goal setting as another tool to berate or criticise oneself. Consider it a step in the right direction. Utilise it as a stepping stone on the path to goal success, enhanced self-esteem, and rewards.

Do not get preoccupied with the proper method of goal-setting or the proper procedure. Avoid engaging in anything that can prompt you to have unfavourable thoughts about yourself. If you allow it, anything might serve as an excuse for you to think adversely about anything. Writing down your objectives is the one and only step of the procedure that you will be required to complete. You have to put them in writing. If you don't put things in writing, you won't be able to attain them. When we say "write them down," we don't mean on a smartphone or tablet; we mean in a diary.

If the objectives you establish are not personal to you and do not really important to you, then you will lack the motivation to work towards achieving them. Create optimistic ideas about your objectives, including what they will accomplish for you and the ways in which you might enhance your life if you are successful in achieving them.

Accomplish Your Objectives and Reward Yourself

It is impossible for us to overstate how essential it is to your sense of pride and competence in yourself that you accomplish these objectives and give yourself a reward for doing so. If you are concerned about your self-esteem, it is best to avoid setting any objectives at all rather than to establish goals for yourself and then fail to achieve them. After you have accomplished them, you should give yourself a reward for your hard work. This is also quite significant. Make sure that you include positive affirmations as a component of that reward system, and make sure that you keep reminding yourself what a fantastic achievement this is.

The Synopsis and the Game Plan

- If you haven't already started one, get yourself a diary dedicated to building your self-esteem right now. Make use of that diary as the area where you chronicle your affirmations, review your objectives, and put them down in writing.

- Please respond to these questions in the most forthright manner possible. It will give you a lot of insight into how you function and will show you what kinds of affirmations and objectives you need to set for yourself.

What actions have you taken in the past that you now wish you hadn't?

What are some things that you have done in the past that you do not feel guilty about?

How often do you catch yourself saying something critical to yourself during the day?

How often do you catch yourself thinking something bad about yourself that you don't actually voice?

How often do you find yourself saying "I can't" in a single day?

Be trustworthy. Be truthful in your responses, even if they make you feel uneasy. Feel free to express whatever emotion you want in response to this, but remember to take stock of how you're affected before moving on. After you have put them down on paper, you will discover that you are more at ease with the answers as well as with yourself.

• Always have an upbeat and optimistic attitude. We have spoken about the concept of positive self-talk; nevertheless, if you really want to enhance your self-esteem, you will want to speak favourably to yourself at all times. Make your house into a fortress of happy ideas. I know this may seem corny, but it's important. Place post-it notes or posters about the home that include motivational quotes or positive affirmations. Continue making adjustments to the messages so that they do not get stale. Get rid of those who are always finding fault with everything. And try to surround yourself solely with people who have a good outlook on life, since this will help to reinforce the thinking patterns you already have.

Do You Consider Yourself To Be A Pessimist?

In the end, it's possible that you're a pessimistic person. You may not be aware of it just yet, but after going through that list up there, you could already have an inkling of what it is. If you get the feeling that you can connect to a lot of those different things, you can come to the conclusion that you are, in fact, a pessimistic person.

You will need to engage in some self-reflection if you want to determine whether or not you are a negative person. How often do you allow emotions of negativity to hold you back? How frequently do you believe that the way you feel is preventing you from achieving your goals? How closely do you identify with the items on the list that was just given to you? How often do you have feelings like that?

Again, keep in mind that it's natural and good to have certain negative emotions throughout your life. There is no need to be embarrassed about it since it is something that occurs on sometimes. That is the kind of thing that occurs on sometimes, and you will be well within your rights to accept it and find a way to make it work for you. As long as you have a healthy mix of positive and negative ideas in your head, it shouldn't be too difficult for you to come to terms with that particular issue.

It may come as a surprise to learn this, but in order to be considered a positive person, it is necessary for you to be thinking around 80% positive thoughts on a daily basis. Which is to imply that you get a free pass for every one in five ideas that you have; if you are thinking negatively around 20% of the time, you are probably doing great; you will be considered a positive person if you think about things more positively than you do negatively. If, on the other hand, you discover that you have a greater number of negative ideas than that, or if you see that the proportion of positive to negative thoughts in your head is about the same, you may in fact be a negative person, and there is no way to dispute that assertion. To your relief, however, if you are able to recognise these unfavourable ideas and make an effort to counteract them, you will discover that it is in fact possible for you to become the upbeat and optimistic person that you have always aspired to be.

Why is being negative so detrimental to you?

When you focus on the negative, it makes you irritable. It makes you feel grumpy, which, regrettably, has a negative impact on your physical health as well.

Families, friendships, and other connections are all susceptible to being destroyed and negatively impacted by negative energy.

You are well aware that being exposed to negativity may cause you to get upset, and as you well know, anger can cause you to act in ways that you will most likely come to regret in the future.

Your brain is impacted when you're unhappy. According to professionals in the field of public health, concentrating on negative thoughts, even for a short period of time (such as thirty minutes), may kill neurons in your brain, more especially in your neurocampus, which is the portion of your brain that is in charge of your ability to solve problems.

The primary issue with thinking negatively is that, in most cases, it does not lead to beneficial results. It will not encourage the development of behaviours that are, in fact, constructive or conducive to success if it does not get anything done, and it does not address what the issue was in the first place. When you allow yourself to be governed by negativity, you are setting yourself up for a life of misery, and just as negativity may spread inside your own mind, you can also transfer it to others. In point of fact, many individuals, when confronted with a negative person, are frequently advised to break off all contact with that person totally, so putting a stop to the cycle of negativity and preventing themselves from being influenced by that negativity and starting to act upon it themselves.

Thinking negatively will not assist you in finding solutions to your difficulties. If you believe that nothing you could possibly do will actually fix the problem at hand, then why would you spend the time and energy attempting to fix it when you see the attempts to fix it as nothing but a waste of the mentioned energy, which is limited and therefore valuable? Negative thinking does nothing but paralyse you. If you believe that nothing you could possibly do will actually fix the problem at hand, then why would you spend the time and energy attempting to fix it? You most likely would not do that; rather, you would focus that energy on something else that is more practical and really makes more sense to bring about the outcome that you want to see occur. Unfortuitously, when you have a sad mind frame that is riddled with negativity, you are not likely to perceive everything as worthy of receiving that focus and effort, and you may not even see everything as worthy of getting attention at all. Instead of taking action, you will choose to take no action.

The conclusion that it is pointless to try since nothing will change is, of course, the final and self-defeating consequence of this line of thought. If you take no action to bring about the transformation you want, you should not be surprised if you do not see any kind of shift in your circumstances. The fact that you were the one who caused it to occur guarantees that there will be unhappiness in the future. Consider it in this light: if you work to solve an issue, there is a possibility that things will become better as a result of your efforts. On the other hand, if you don't even attempt, you give yourself a 100% chance of failing. You can never know for sure if something is impossible or whether it will turn out a particular way if you never attempt it or put yourself in harm's path.

Consider it from this perspective: the detrimental assumption that you have about yourself is that you have no value. You have convinced yourself that you are incapable of achieving success in your professional life because you are not valuable. since of this mindset, you do not apply for the job that you would be reasonably good at, and since you do not really apply for the job, you will never get the opportunity to demonstrate that you are capable of being excellent at your work. You were unable to acquire a job because you convinced yourself that you would never be qualified for any position, which only adds fuel to the fire of your pessimistic outlook on life.

On the other side, your negative ideas can appear at some point in time to further emphasise the beliefs that you have been clinging to. For instance, if you have the mindset that you aren't worth anything, and then you apply for a job and are turned down for it, you can consider that experience as evidence that your negative thoughts are correct. You say to yourself that it is not surprising that you were not chosen for the job since you are useless. Because you were not selected for the job, you feel that the negative ideas that have been going through your head are somewhat justified. You could convince yourself that you are to blame for failing at your job or that there is no way that you could ever possible succeed in the same manner that your coworkers are. As a result, you would find it difficult to see the value in continuing or even trying, which would once again contribute to the perpetuation of the cycle of self-defeating, negative ideas.

Altering Feelings Via Changes In Behavior

When you take into consideration the James-Lange hypothesis, you are left with the type of equation that looks like this and it equals emotions:

Stimulus plus the body's response plus the mind's interpretation equals emotion.

You can use this to your advantage by manipulating it. You could use this to break any form of bad emotional patterns, such as becoming upset and screaming, which simply makes you get more angrier, or you could use it to stop a phobia via exposure, reminders that you are safe and okay, deep breaths, and lots of patience on your part. You are able to control how you feel by changing the things you do, so the possibilities are almost endless. The only thing you need to do to modify the way you feel about a certain stimulus is to adjust both your bodily reaction and how you perceive that reaction as it relates to the stimulus.

Take, for instance, the experience of going through a divorce as an illustration. The mere appearance of your ex-spouse when exchanging custody of your children is enough to make your blood boil, and regardless of what you do or the circumstances under which you encounter your ex-spouse, you are unable to prevent yourself from being instantly outraged. Perhaps he cheated on you or did something else that made such a profound imprint on you that you experience the feeling instantly and to such a great extent at the mere sight of him. This may be the case.

You should be ready for the next time you are going to visit your ex-spouse so that you don't feel unprepared. You are going to take a deep breath the moment you see him. You will posture yourself to be tall and upright. Your shoulders will become more relaxed. You are going to engage in calm eye contact with him. You will not speak louder than necessary. You won't get all worked up over it. You are going to maintain steady, deep, and slow breathing throughout this exercise, counting to four between each breath if necessary. Make a plan for what you will do the next time you have to switch custody of someone with another person by making a list of the steps you will do. After all, you are aware that it is harmful for your children to see you harbouring hatred against their father, and you do not want to subject them to that experience.

Therefore, when you go back to that location, you should make it a point to try all of the activities listed above. It is going to be challenging. You are going to have to battle against your gut emotions that are connected to your anger for the guy who deceived you, but as you do this, you will discover that you are gaining control of the situation as well as yourself. You will have the ability to coax yourself into a condition of serenity, in which you will be able to exert self-control.

Imagine then that you come face to face with him. You start to feel your blood pressure rise and your pulse start to beat as you become acutely aware of the well-known sensation of wrath rising up inside of you to the point that you worry that you could burst into flames. You decide to pause what you're doing rather than giving in to the wrath and the tension that are rapidly gaining control of your body. You temporarily cover your eyes with your hands. You inhale deeply, count to four, and then hold your breath for as long as you can. By doing this, you are not only calming yourself down but also filtering off the physical input that is making you angry. Your peripheral nervous system is stimulated whenever you take a breath in and then hold it for a period of time. Your heart receives a signal to slow down as a result of this. It is reading your lack of breathing as a need to preserve oxygen, which is done by beating less often. This is done because you have stopped breathing. It slows down because the more it beats, the more oxygen it requires, thus the cycle continues. It is sufficient on its own to have a relaxing effect. After that, you may work on releasing the tension in your shoulders by starting to shrug them. You should take a few slow, deep breaths and try to relax even more. In the end, you will feel that wrath melting away little by little, leaving behind your calm condition that is ready to confront your spouse without anger or rage. This state will allow you to approach your spouse without anger or rage.

Altering your emotions may be done in a number of different ways; however, the most common technique is to transition from a state of agitation, anxiety, or grief into a state of calm and levelheadedness. This provides you with the opportunity to further evaluate your situation and surroundings in order to behave in a manner that is acceptable. By using the endorphins produced during exercise, you may induce feelings of pleasure or contentment in yourself. You may also induce patience by controlling your breathing and your body language.

What Is Self Confidence?

Confidence is the phrase that we use to characterise our own evaluation of our competence or capacity to carry out a job, function, or position that we have been assigned. When you claim that you are positive that you will do really well in that interview, you are implying that you are almost certain that you will be successful. It is an assessment of your talents, including your ability to attain objectives you have set for yourself, find solutions to difficulties, and think independently. Does this imply that self-confidence and self-esteem are synonymous concepts, despite the fact that we often use these terms interchangeably in a variety of contexts?

Confidence in oneself as opposed to self-esteem

Even though they are often used interchangeably, self-confidence and self-esteem refer to two separate concepts that are not equivalent in any way.

What exactly is self-esteem, then?

There is a strong correlation between self-esteem and self-worth, which may be defined as the value that one places on themselves. Ask yourself, "How comfortable am I being me?" in order to evaluate your sense of self-worth. How much do I believe I am worthy of joy and success in my life? Your sincere responses to these and other questions of a similar kind will help you to calculate the value that you put upon yourself.

Your feeling of belonging, or the degree to which you believe that you are accepted and appreciated by other people, is another component of your overall sense of self-worth. The term "others" refers to key people in your life whose opinions you respect, such as members of your family or coworkers at your place of employment.

Therefore, how you feel about yourself, how you appear, how you think, and whether or not you feel valued all contribute to your overall level of self-esteem. It has an underlying quality of "otherness" mostly due to the fact that your self-esteem is composed of the experiences and interpersonal interactions you have had throughout your life. Everyone you've ever been in contact with has either contributed to or detracted from how you now feel about yourself.

What exactly is self-confidence, then?

On the other hand, self-confidence may be defined as a belief in oneself and one's own skills.

What is the first thing that springs to mind when you hear someone say, "I am confident about abc but..." or "I am fully confident that I will..."? Both of these hypothetical situations suggest that varying degrees of assurance are possible. Let's get some additional information about these levels.

Measures of Confidence

Your degree of self-confidence will fluctuate depending on the day of the week and the circumstances you find yourself in. Our degree of confidence in our abilities to carry out tasks might fluctuate, and although some days you may feel more confident than others, this is not always the case. These variations are sometimes caused by the circumstances that are currently present, such as your level of expertise in a task, familiarity with a role or the people involved, the gravity of the situation, such as facing a job interview panel as opposed to learning how to prepare a new dish, and your emotional stability, to name a few of these factors.

In most cases, the amount of self-confidence is noticeable not just to you as the role player but also to others around you. This is due to the fact that it is possible to infer from the way you carry yourself and your body language. Whether you are conscious of it or not, the way you carry yourself, such as with fluid motions, a quick pitchy tone, a hard dry handshake, level gaze, or hunched shoulders, all have something to do with your confidence.

Given that there are varying degrees of confidence, does this imply that it is possible to have an extreme amount of either low or high levels of confidence?

*Is it possible to have an excessive amount of self-assurance?

An excessive amount of self-confidence sometimes comes off as arrogance, especially when it's shown in the form of feeling or acting superior to other people. Aggressive behaviour may be triggered by having a strong feeling of entitlement and overvaluing one's own achievements in comparison to those of others. To combat this, it is important to keep in mind that regardless of how successful you are or how talented you are, you are not flawless. In fact, just like everyone else, you have a balanced set of talents, flaws, and failures.Is it conceivable to have an insufficient amount of self-confidence?

The overwhelming response to this question is yes. Yes! A significant portion of us struggle with insecurity, often known as lack of confidence or poor self-confidence.

Here are some of the behaviours that are often associated with either high or low levels of self-confidence, in order to assist you in making the distinction between the two. What kinds of mental processes and behaviours do you see both in yourself and in other people? It is possible for you to establish whether or not your degree of self-confidence is healthy by first gaining an understanding of the behaviours that you are likely to display in relation to your self-confidence.

How To Make Yourself The Centre Of Attention In Your Own Life

A significant number of individuals go through life without ever establishing for themselves any worthwhile personal standards. They don't live up to their potential and wind up playing a supporting role in their own life, despite the fact that they should be just as great, courageous, honourable, and intelligent as the main character. Even if it goes without saying that reality is nothing like the movies, that does not mean that you should stop trying to be "The One" who comes through in the clutch and saves the day.

How can one develop the self-assurance necessary to make themselves the central figure in their own life stories? You are going to proceed in the following manner:

First, make the conscious decision to improve your situation. Nobody else—not your parents, not your coworkers, nor even your spouse—is in command of your life.

Be aware that you are going to be your closest buddy during your time spent in this earth. Even if there is no doubting the significance of the connections you have, the only things you really have are your ideas, actions, and choices. When you make the decision to start taking responsibility for yourself, you will almost immediately see a major shift in perspective.

Step 2: Express in words exactly what it is that you want to accomplish in your life.

Say it out loud to yourself and get it into your head that you can do whatever it is you want to accomplish. You are announcing to both yourself and the universe that you are about to go on a trip with the end objective of accomplishing something. Reaching this objective will give you the sense that you have made the most of your time here on earth.

The third step is to get moving!

Prepare yourself with a detailed strategy, and make the most of the resources you have. Take something useful away from each day, bearing in mind that errors and setbacks may be some of the finest lessons. Appreciate and rely on the assistance of your close pals. Get advice and guidance from your mentors. First and foremost, you should never take the time that is happening right now for granted since you can never get that moment back after it has already gone.

Get clear on what it is that you desire and take the initiative to guide yourself to fulfilment of those aspirations. Devote some time each day to inspiring yourself and keeping yourself on the correct path. First and foremost, remember to enjoy yourself while doing it. When you zero in on the things in life that are actually important to you and go to work pursuing those goals, confidence won't be far after.

Increasing One's Self-Assurance

People that have difficulties with their self-esteem tend to exaggerate things, which is one of the problems of having these issues. They do not act in this manner consciously; rather, it is just how they cope with life's challenges. Consider this: if you make a mistake, what is the very worst thing that may happen? You see it as an act of humiliation and as more evidence that you are not enough for the task at hand. Nothing of the kind is true, and if you believe otherwise, it is because you have a problem with your own self-esteem. Failures of today become something that people laugh about the day after they occur.

If you believe that you are a failure at anything, the first step towards building confidence is to take tiny measures towards improving your performance. The most effective strategy for boosting one's self-assurance is to ensure that one spends a sufficient amount of time engaging in activities that one is already proficient at. Everyone has qualities that they excel in, and even those who struggle with low self-esteem and lack of confidence will have some areas in which they shine. Sitting down with a sheet of paper in front of you and writing down the activities that you take pleasure in performing is the most effective method for determining which employment are suitable for you. The majority of the time, the reason why activities are enjoyable to individuals is because they are inside their comfort zones. For instance, I find pleasure in cooking and am well aware of my skills in that area. Even if your preferences are completely different, using them as a jumping off point will help you build confidence.

Because doing well at things may make you feel more confident, you should try to spend a considerable portion of each day focusing on activities in which you excel. The reason why this works is because if you are engaging in activities that you are familiar with for fifty percent of the time, then it constitutes fifty percent positive input for your levels of confidence. Be careful to choose activities that you take pleasure in performing and that can easily be included into your routine.

I can tell you that during the first week of writing articles for a publication, I was wringing my hands, yelling in my room, and shivering from nervousness. I can tell you this because I can remember doing all of those things. The task was quite difficult, and there was a significant amount of information that needed to be produced in a relatively short amount of time. My ability to handle time poorly was one of my weaknesses. Although I was acquainted with the subject matter I was writing about, I did not have a knowledge foundation that was substantial enough to allow me to seamlessly fulfil the demands of the timetable. Since I was a young child, I have been terrified of deadlines and have done all in my power to avoid them. As a result, my academic performance in college suffered, and my reputation suffered at subsequent jobs. I really like the flexibility that the article work offered, since it gave me the opportunity to set my own schedule and decide, to some degree, what I wanted to write about. In spite of this, when I was under such a great deal of pressure, I couldn't shake the feeling that I was beyond my ability, and I wanted nothing more than to throw in the towel and give up because I was so frustrated and afraid of failing.

Writing is something I like doing, and I found that working as a freelance writer allowed me the flexibility and experience I needed to create a successful career as a writer. Therefore, rather of giving in to my fear of failing and feeling of self-defeat, which were stifling my confidence, I made the decision to continue pursuing one of my loves despite these negative emotions.

However, I came to the realisation that my approach to the work as well as my mindset on deadlines needed to be revised. When I decided to do some independent research into the company I was going to be working for, that was the moment when things began to turn around for me. I did some research on other authors who had achieved success and the advice they had to give. For the purpose of helping me stay on target, remain focused, and create consistency, I began keeping track of the hours during which I worked as well as the moments during which I took breaks or allowed myself to be distracted. When it came to article subjects that I did not know enough about, I ensured that I allowed myself a sufficient amount of time in advance to do as much research as I could on the subject. This ensured that the material that I wrote was current and would flow more smoothly when it was put into practise.

My progress in my practise was bolstered by each of these factors, which were all of great assistance to me. I was able to reclaim some of my lost self-confidence, which was quite encouraging. On the other hand, I saw that I was still falling short of the goal when it came to meeting those pesky deadlines. I saw that even though I was making progress towards being more efficient in my work, I was still getting stressed out by the mere concept of working under a deadline, and when I was in that stressed-out condition, I would constantly delay from completing my job. I observed that even though I was making progress towards being more efficient in my work, I was still feeling stressed. Because of the tension at work, I had a hard time concentrating on my job, and the ideas I had for the essay came to me in fits and starts while I was there. My performance was being gently hindered by all of those suppressed memories of when I had failed in the past, both in school and at previous employment. My sense of self-worth took yet another knock, and I found that I was beginning to question my abilities once again.

It was fortunate for my obstinate nature that I was resolved to see it through to the end. I came to the realisation that I needed to alter my thinking once again, but this time in a manner that was far more terrifying than the last. I had to directly address my fear of failing, which I had been living with and trying to escape for such a long time. What was my secret to success? Well, one thing that helped was that I had been working on many of the activities listed in this book including meditation, positive affirmations, and negative thought observation for several years, which helped me to shift in other aspects of my life. This book includes exercises like those. I had the appropriate resources available to me, and it was time to put them to use in order to address one of the most critical challenges that was preventing me from realising one of my aspirations. I had been putting this off long enough. I was also aware that if I worked on resolving this problem in this specific aspect of my life, the advantages that resulted from doing so would spread into other aspects of my life in which I felt like I was being held back. Simply being aware of it and believing it with every fibre of my being contributed to my improved mood and provided a modest lift to my self-assurance.

It was necessary for me to convince myself that I am not a loser. I reminded myself that I am a strong person for going for my goal despite all of the setbacks and disappointments that I have encountered. I stared in the mirror at myself or sought a quiet location where I told myself how much I love myself. I expressed gratitude to myself for seizing this opportunity in my life to make positive changes and assured myself that I would be successful because I like writing, I am excellent at it, and I would not give up striving to improve myself in this area. This was something that I performed for fifteen minutes each day in the beginning of the day, when I was most tempted to avoid getting started on my job, as well as during breaks in the middle of my work. Whenever I noticed the stress level rising while I was working, I would stop what I was doing for only five minutes to perform some breathing exercises or a meditation activity to help clear my mind. This helped me feel more in control of the situation. I also switched from drinking a lot of coffee and eating a lot of sweets to eating a lot more fruits and vegetables since I knew this would have a far more beneficial effect on my energy levels. I also removed a two-hour chunk of my daily routine so that I could do some cardiovascular training in addition to working on my stretching and breathing. I was aware that this would improve my circulation and give my body more energy, which would result in a clearer mind and the sense of accomplishment that comes from knowing you are taking care of both your body and your mind. My normal morning ritual got the day off to a good start and mentally prepared me for an enjoyable and fruitful day of work.

This did not take place all at once by any stretch of the imagination. I had to put each routine into place piece by piece over the course of approximately a month, and even when I had achieved some level of consistency with each of them, it took me another couple of months to get everything to work together smoothly. When I felt the first signs of stress, I would use it as a barometer and a reminder to participate in one of these practises. I did this as soon as I could. If there was one thing that kept me going, it was the knowledge that it did not seem right to let stress get the best of me or to give up on doing something that I loved. I was bound and determined to discover the positive aspects of myself. In all seriousness, who wouldn't be?

Because I had redirected my attention to these productive practises, I had completely forgotten about the approaching deadlines. In addition, by continuing to engage in these activities for short bursts of ten to fifteen minutes here and there, I was able to significantly reduce the amount of stress I felt and significantly increase the amount of work I got done. I was able to recover my self-assurance in a graceful manner, and when I considered all that I had accomplished, I found that I could not stop smiling. To this day, I still go around with a grin on my face, and on occasion, I notice that other people are also smiling as a result of their observation of me.

It is important to keep in mind that you do not have to depend only on your own resources in order to bring about the change in yourself that you want. Share your plans with the people in your close circle of friends and family in whom you have complete faith, and solicit their assistance. Ask them to check in with you at regular intervals to see how you are doing and let you know how they did. When you feel like you need it, you may even request that they assist you in remaining focused on the work at hand. Your friends and family will undoubtedly be willing to support you in your time of need. Be wary if you don't know anything or have any doubts about it. That is a pessimistic way of thinking, and all it does is prevent you from moving forward. You will never know the actual answer until you ask. You may as well give it a go since there is nothing to lose (and this is the mentality that we are looking for here because it is so empowering for individuals to achieve their objectives), so don't be afraid to share your thoughts. It's possible that you'll be pleasantly pleased.

Overcoming Unproductive And Negative Thoughts

Everyone has a creative side, even if it is sometimes hidden and doesn't come to the surface as quickly as it does for other people. However, you can cultivate your creative side by digging for hidden potential and working on it, searching for your innovative side and bringing it to the forefront of your life. The following are some helpful hints that will assist you in cultivating your creative capabilities and developing your inventive spirit.

• Make lists - producing a list will help you considerably expand your imagination and get that part of your brain going. Whenever you have a problem that requires some innovative speculation, write down as many ideas as you can for potential solutions and let your creative juices to flow freely. This will allow your imagination to grow significantly.

• Implement alterations all through your life – if we are stuck in a dismal cycle, sometimes we are able to have a creative block; if you want to get the channels flowing once more, implement specific alterations all throughout your life.

• Work on the ill-conceived ideas – even if you are only thinking of impractical ideas, you are still being imaginative, so give the terrible ones a shot and create them. Who's to say that it's an ill-conceived idea anyway? It might turn out to be an incredible idea and the solution to your problems.

• Collaborate with others in an excellent - collaborating with others and generating ideas at the same time while working in a group is an incredible way to innovate.

• Put yourself and other people to the test. If you put yourself to the test by telling yourself that you can't complete a task in the manner in which you have always completed it, you will be forced to consider alternative means of resolving the problem, which may result in some very original ideas. If you put other people to the test, you will be forced to think creatively about how to solve the problem.

• If you are stuck for ideas to an answer, then have a pen and paper handy and doodle your thoughts on the paper. It is astonishing what you will think of if you free your mind in this manner. If you are stuck for ideas to an answer, then doodle your thoughts on the paper.

- Stimulate the part of your brain that is responsible for thinking - the left side of your brain is where your imagination is born, so give it a jolt and wake it up by acting with the right half of your brain. You can also try inhaling through only your left nostril a few times to see if it makes a difference.

- Employ a holistic mentor – If you believe that your innovativeness has reached its limit, you should think about enlisting the assistance of a holistic mentor to help you think that it is. A holistic mentor can assist you in determining the areas in which your imagination is lacking and will work with you to strengthen it.

- Think like a child – Put aside all of your adult responsibilities, stresses, strains, and stresses and return to your youth. Children have the most brilliant minds, and their imaginations are boundless. Adopt the mindset of a child when you are at a loss for creative ideas, and you will find that they will come to you uninhibitedly in due time.

• Take some time to relax - being under a great deal of stress can sometimes cause our creative juices to run dry. Learning how to relax properly not only helps you feel better, but it can also help clear your mind, give you a fresh start, and get your creative juices flowing again.

• Use some mind games - have a handful of mind games on hand, such as logic puzzles. By getting your mind off your issue and focusing on solving a riddle, you are engaging in attentive thinking, which in turn encourages constructive and creative thought.

Advice and options for creative endeavours

Everyone has the potential to improve their life by engaging in creative endeavours. You may use your creativity to assist with a variety of different things, like managing projects at work, establishing goals, managing your house and family, and a lot more. Here are ten suggestions to help you become more creative, which should be useful in the bulk of the projects you do, both at home and at work.

1. Take Care of Your Body

Find a routine of activities that you like doing and commit to doing them regularly. Alter it as necessary, but keep up with some kind of the activity that you were doing before. Get some good rest. Consume a wide variety of nutritious foods and drinks. You may help keep your thoughts centred by engaging in activities like contemplation or activities that you like doing to relax.

2. Attempt Unfamiliar Activities

We are able to do such a vast range of things without giving them any thought. These activities get ingrained in our daily routines, becoming them mundane and taxing on our bodies. Try your hand at something completely different. It is very possible that it will be anything as little as taking a different route to work or doing something like enrolling in an additional class to study something that has been on your mind for a considerable amount of time.

3. Begin to Think in the Way That Curious George Does

Put everything that you see, hear, and read into perspective by engaging in introspective questioning. Why? And if not, then how? Find out the answers to the questions you've asked. Additionally, you have the option of maintaining an investigative journal in which you may record all of your findings.

4. Start a Brand-New Book 4.

Choose the option that you typically wouldn't go with. You may get a copy from the library. Even if you've always been more interested in real-world information, you should read some fiction at some point. There is such a vast amount of fascinating books to read, and as a result, there is a diverse selection of types to look over. When it comes to looking into new books, the person who is responsible for the library will be happy to help you.

5. Pretend You're a Youngster

Children are full of innocence, sincerity, and pleasure. Think back to the things you used to do when you were younger that had no specific point or purpose. Anything that a youngster might be interested in doing, such as painting a picture, getting out the charcoals, getting some finger paints, going to a local event congregation, etc. In addition to that, I hope you have a wonderful time!

6. It's Important for Everyone to Have Some "Personal" Time

Make it a habit to give yourself regular time to just relax. If you like thinking, you could benefit from engaging in some reflective thinking. Make every effort to avoid making any plans, paying any bills, or doing anything else. To put it simply, it won't help for very long. 7. What If It Were?

What would happen if tomorrow was the end of the world? Consider for a moment that you attended a school that specialised in business. Think about the likelihood that those from the outside were telling the truth. Think about the idea that there is another life beyond this one. Create your own questions, picture a situation in which they apply, and then sit back and see where your imagination takes you.

8. Make no presumptions about anything.

Expecting anything may often lead to unpleasant outcomes for the one doing the expecting. You probably anticipate that your boss will be easy to work with. Imagine a situation in which he just doesn't care about his life and takes it out on his employees instead of seeking help for himself. You may probably assume that the person who cut you off at the beginning of today was impolite because of their behaviour. Consider the possibility that they were rushing their child to the emergency room of a nearby hospital.

9. Describe Yourself in Writing

Who are you, exactly? In your own words, what kind of person would you say you are? Where have you spent the most of your life up to this point? When are the most important things that have happened to you during your life? Why do you conduct yourself in the way in which you do all that you do? What steps would you take to get through each day of your life?

10. Engage in Conversations with Other Individuals

Instead of assuming it will be your time to speak, focus on what the other person has to say and actively listen to what they have to say. What does it look like to be this particular individual? Imagine what their daily life is like and how they think.

Both Strengths And Challenges Characterise Highly Sensitive Introverts.

Empaths possess a great lot of qualities that enable them to live full and lovely lives and provide support for them in doing so. It will be much simpler for you to bring your empathic ability into line with the rest of your life after you have begun to accept your identity as an empath and have included self-protection and self-care practises into your daily routine. This indicates that you may start taking use of the various advantages and benefits that come with being an empath.

When you awaken to your empathic skills and start to take control over them, you may look forward to growing and embodying many great qualities. Here are some of the strengths that you can look forward to developing and embodying:

A Major World Power

The power of empaths should not be underestimated. This is one of the many reasons why people in society look down on them so much. They are terrified of the power that they have. You are clearly not like the normal person because you have the ability to pick up on things about other people that they may not be ready to talk about or because you have the ability to form profound connections with the plants and animals in your environment. In today's contemporary civilization, there are a significant number of people who live their lives in complete isolation from the rest of the world. They have difficulty tuning in on even the most fundamental levels, much less going as in-depth as you do. It's possible that you see it as a weakness, but that's only because you've been socialised to think that way. In point of fact, you have a significant amount of authority. You will be unstoppable in your efforts to bring about good change in the world once you have learned to accept it and work to your advantage by using it.

An Incredible Acquaintance

Anyone who counts an Empath among their circle of friends ought to feel an overwhelming sense of gratitude. People that are empathic are wonderful companions. Those who are empathic have a profound affection for the people in their lives that they care about and would go to any extent to support and safeguard them. They are able to provide excellent counsel to their buddies. When a friend is dealing with a challenge of some kind, empaths are pleased to put their wonderful gift of empathy to work by imagining what it would be like to be in their friend's position in order to have a better understanding of the circumstance and to determine what the most appropriate course of action would be.

Capability of Identifying Warning Signs

You have an incredible capacity to recognise warning signs in any individual or circumstance, thanks to your unique perspective that allows you to see what's going on under the surface of things. You may do this by empathising with the other person, which effectively enables you to put yourself in their position. This indicates that you are able to recognise the consistency that exists between the individual's words, actions, and emotions. There, you will be able to ascertain whether or not they are behaving in a manner that is congruent with the truth, whether or not they are lying, or whether or not they are dishonest in any way. You are able to determine whether or not there is a covert agenda at play when you recognise any symptoms of incongruence.

It is an entirely separate matter whether or not you choose to really recognise and act on them, but the fact that you are able to detect them and become aware of them is a very powerful talent on its own. If you are tuned in and able to act on the information that you get, it will be simple for you to avoid danger and energetic assaults. Because you are able to recognise whenever there is anything intrinsically incorrect with a situation, it will be easy for you to avoid both danger and energetic attacks. If you are not yet, there is no need for alarm. Because you are an empath, you have the power to access this skill whenever you choose. You still have time to make a change.

Finding People Who Lie All the Time

You have the capacity to swiftly identify those who are habitually dishonest, which is yet another advantageous skill you possess as a result of your keen insight into the inner workings of other people. You can tell very immediately when other individuals are lying to you. You can identify the harmony between the person's words, actions, and emotions in the same way as you can notice the red flags. If you are able to identify any indicators of discord, it will be much simpler for you to think that someone is lying. This often manifests itself as little more than a "knowingness" inside. This provides you with the motivation to avoid from believing them and may assist you in stopping yourself from being sucked into and caught up in the web of falsehoods that they have spun. The more you put effort into developing this skill, the more effectively you will be able to use your talent.

If you are a wounded healer who is unable to make effective use of your gift, you may discover that you are drawn into another person's web of falsehoods. In the process of mending this archetype, if you have it, this is something that has to be addressed, since it is vital.

Powerful abilities in the creative arts

People that have a natural talent for something It is common knowledge that empaths are blessed with exceptional creative abilities. They are very competent artists, singers, poets, authors, and creators in general, as was previously said in this conversation. Empaths have a poetic way of seeing the world, which allows them to produce one-of-a-kind works of art that showcase their own perspective on the world. It is quite remarkable how they are able to imagine something in their heads and then bring it into the physical world via the use of their imagination. The majority of empaths will struggle the hardest when it comes to releasing all of the negative energy that they have taken in over their lives. This pessimism may manifest itself in uncertainties such as doubt, insecurity, fear of failing, and a general lack of confidence.

Although there are a variety of ways in which empaths might express or make use of their creative potential, almost all empaths have the ability to be creative. To put it another way, not every empath will be exceptionally talented in the same areas, but they will all have some degree of creative potential that they may tap into to express who they are and how they want to contribute to the world. This provides the Empath with a sense of immense fulfilment and satisfaction.

Excellent at finding solutions to problems.

When an empath has developed their innate ability to feel what others are experiencing, they are in a position to be exceptional problem solvers. Because of their capacity for empathy, they are in a position to examine the desires and requirements of many parties from a variety of perspectives. Because empaths are able to examine a given circumstance and see it from a variety of perspectives, they have a significant advantage when it comes to finding a solution that will be helpful to all sides of a conflict and will be a win-win for everyone involved.

4.4 The Relationship

A significant number of us lead lives that are far too secluded. You shouldn't go against the natural and healthy need that all humans have, which is to desire to congregate with other people; doing so would be counterproductive. At this point in time, you probably have a love partner, friends, and perhaps even family. However, a large number of individuals do not or cannot fit into any of these groups. Let's have a conversation about each of them.

The first, an intimate or romantic connection, is often a cause of tension and unhappiness for a great number of individuals. A lot of individuals experience feelings of loneliness and have the impression that it is impossible to meet someone who is interested in dating them. It's possible that they'll isolate themselves from the rest of the world. One further example is that sometimes these individuals are cut off from the rest of the world as a result of certain biases that exist in the world and certain ways that we expect people to behave. The fact that other individuals have too many connections is the root source of their troubles. They are skilled at making new acquaintances and tracking down individuals, but they struggle when it comes to handling romantic partnerships. They'll get into a relationship that isn't good for them and do things merely to maintain their status in the relationship.

These individuals are often referred to as codependents. Codependents take pleasure in seeing another person suffer since it mirrors their own state of being. They do not enjoy the feeling of being vulnerable and want things to continue operating normally and under their control. People who are codependent often find methods to maintain unhealthy relationships, typically out of fear that they won't have anybody to rely on if they leave the unhealthy relationship. They often lack a sense of identity, and as a result, it is relatively simple for them to get entangled in the lives of others and in love relationships. Codependent individuals are not adept at living on their own and would rather be in an unhealthy relationship than have no connection at all. Codependent people would rather be in an unhealthy relationship than have no relationship at all.

People who fall into either of these categories, avoiders or codependents, will need to acquire the skill of learning to open up in order to successfully form new relationships. They face unique obstacles based on the characteristics of their personalities, but this should be their overarching objective: to become more open and to cultivate more meaningful relationships.

The individual who is an introvert or who often enjoys their own company more than being with others will need to learn how to open up and be able to put oneself in circumstances where they are socialising and having fun with other people. It may seem strange or odd at first for the introvert, but the more a person is exposed to social circumstances, the more comfortable they will feel with themselves in such situations.

Anecdote showing a typical progression of events in terms of land development in this region is shown below. It's not the case that everyone's life will play out exactly like this, but it's a situation that's quite likely to happen. Mark is a male resident of the province of Ontario. Mark had a childhood that was fairly conventional in the sense that he grew up in a suburban town and participated in the traditional activities for a kid growing up in his neighbourhood. However, Mark eventually came to the realisation that he was not able to interact to other people as effectively as he would have wanted to have been able to. In addition to having frequent arguments with one another, Mark's parents were also terrible at maintaining friendships. They would often mope about the home, getting into disputes or otherwise behaving in a hostile and irritable manner. Friendships did not seem to be a part of the model of life that Mark's parents projected to him, so he learnt to avoid other people and to not trust anybody. Mark learned this since his parents did not value the importance of friendships in their own lives. Friendships were an optional bonus, something you might pursue if you had the time, but in most cases, they were only a side note.

Mark began his senior year of high school and immediately became involved with a group of students who were intellectually capable but enjoyed getting into mischief. They would slip into the restrooms at lunch in order to evade their duties for the afternoon, and they wouldn't emerge from the restrooms until the last bell rung. They were known to irritate their instructors on occasion due to their mischievous nature and penchant for stirring the pot. However, with time, the instructors came to see that these children had a high level of intelligence and were just daring.

Mark ultimately received his diploma from high school and enrolled in an art school in Rhode Island for his undergraduate studies. When he first began lessons, he was both eager and frightened, but he was quickly drawn into the art world. He began to socialise with other artists of a similar age, and he eventually felt a sense of belonging in a group. The first genuine step he took towards opening up was when he met one of the other people who were a part of the art group and introduced himself to them. Mark had been out for most of the day, but it was becoming late, and he was on his way back to his hostel. When he looked up from his music on his headphones, he saw a table that had been placed up in front of the art building. He says to himself, "I am not the type of person to go up and introduce myself," but then he does it, and he says to them, "Hi, my name is Mark. I'm from the United Kingdom." I have a deep appreciation for the visual arts, and I am fascinated by what you are doing. They laugh at his naïve demeanour at first, but then they see that he is sincere and they begin to introduce themselves. They conclude that Mark has an interesting outlook on art, and as a result, they would want to have him as a member of the club. It didn't take much for Mark to break out of his initial reservedness and develop relationships in his community; all he needed to do was discover a secondary interest that was related to his primary activity, such as painting.

The development of a close relationship is one of life's most precious gifts. In the beginning, you have a lot of ideas about the person that are based on their manner of talking, the clothing they wear, and their age. The more conversation you have with the other individual, the more you realise that you are compatible with one another. You then begin to spend more time with them, at which point you become aware that you like your time spent with them. After that, you start to perceive them from a little different perspective. When you compare the person you first believed they were to the person they really are, you can find that your first impressions of them were inaccurate. This may lead to some misunderstandings, but in the end it is quite normal. After that, you begin to create a deeper connection with the individual, at which point you become aware that you can trust them. Because you have spent time with them in a variety of settings and are familiar with their behaviour in most circumstances, you have faith in them.

The only thing you need to do to make this happen is to let your guard down and be yourself. In all intimate relationships, there is always an element of concern present. It is the conviction that the other person will or will not support you in times of need.

It is normal for individuals to keep their distance from others. It's something that a lot of folks pick up along the road. In point of fact, one may make the assumption that a very large number of individuals behave in such a manner in order to safeguard themselves. People are walled off because it enables them to escape their feelings, which is preferable than concealing the challenging and excruciating job of dealing with those feelings. When someone is overwhelmed with work and at a loss for what to do next, they may resort to shutting off everything in their life.

Life is not meant to be an endless parade of suffering. There are carnivals in it for sure, and some of them are carnivals of suffering. Some of the carnivals are even fun. You will need to pay in order to participate in these carnivals, but each one has the potential to be entertaining in its own way. On the other hand, those who have a perspective of the world that is too gloomy are doing a disservice to both themselves and others. Everything that goes up eventually has to come back down. There is always a response that is both equal and opposing to the action that was taken. These are the fundamental principles that underpin entropy. According to the theory of entropy, we are now living in a cosmos that is always deteriorating and coming more and more apart. It is a location that will never amount to anything, just as it was before to the beginning of this endeavour. Entropy asserts, in a nutshell, that even if there is a concentration of heat in one section of the room, it will not remain in that location for very long. It will grow in size before finally disappearing completely. It is identical to the whole of the known cosmos. Everything is disintegrating into nothingness slowly. We humans will progress at a far faster rate than the world; the earth had its beginnings a very long time ago and has continued to tick through time since then. The reality of human existence is not so much like that.

In point of fact, a human existence is more comparable to a photograph or a little clip played inside the boundless sea of time that represents nothing more than pitch-blackness in the cinema. It is difficult to comprehend due to its size and the fact that it is so very little. How is it that we are able to experience pure unadulterated delight, ecstasy, and genuine connection at times? What is the significance of anything?

Because no one else can locate the solution for you, it is up to you to come to a conclusion on this matter by yourself. You have to interact with the question and come to your own conclusions about the solutions. However, if you have an open mind and keep searching, there is no way that you won't discover anything to bring you pleasure in this world. There is not the slightest possibility that you will not be happy where you are right now. You are going to discover something. There is a possibility that one evening you may see a sunset that will leave you gasping for air. It may be a piece of film that makes you shed a tear. It has the potential to be a delicious supper. Because finding happiness in this world is essential to what it is to be human, you will eventually figure out how to do so. We all have it inside us, and everyone of us is capable of unearthing it.

Do you have any idea what might make doing it a lot simpler? Allowing yourself to experience what you need to experience with other people and opening yourself up to the possibility of having connections is important. This might refer to relationships with family members, friends, lovers, or others. No matter what it is, you will need to find a way to open your heart to the sort of connections that are involved here, and once you do that, you will discover that you are entirely with another person. To be fully present with another person, you need to give the present moment your undivided attention and really inhabit the moment that you are sharing with that other person. You may find that your thoughts have wandered, and you may experience feelings of distraction or fear; nevertheless, you can always return to the room, and you can always be with yourself and that other person in that same instant.

The Numerous Advantages Of Increasing One's Self-Confidence

When a person boosts their level of self-confidence, they will experience many of the same positive effects as they do when they boost their level of self-esteem. We have reached this stage in the book when we have gained the knowledge that when a person's self-esteem is raised, it also raises that person's level of self-confidence. Since the impacts of self-confidence tend to be more noticeable to others, the advantages of having it also tend to be more apparent to others. People are often capable of concealing their poor self-esteem, but it is far more difficult to conceal their lack of self-confidence. Getting to know someone well enough to have in-depth talks with them and spending a significant amount of time in their company is the best way to determine whether or not someone has low self-esteem. Observing a person's physical posture, level of comfort, and ability to interact socially are three of the easiest ways to determine whether or not they have healthy levels of self-confidence. A person's ability to modify the results of their actions and earn respect from others may be directly correlated to their level of self-confidence. People who operate in environments that emphasise teamwork should prioritise developing their sense of self-assurance. People who are more self-assured are better able to foster an atmosphere at work that is more conducive to collaboration and in which coworkers are encouraged to share their thoughts and ideas rather than blindly following the recommendations of others. In positions of authority, those who are able to articulate their ideas and perspectives in a manner that is respectful of others' sensibilities are in great demand. A greater level of self-confidence comes with a number of advantages, including the following:

Increasing one's level of self-confidence has been shown to enhance a number of aspects of one's life, including overall performance, overall happiness, social abilities, and both one's physical and mental health. Increasing one's level of self-confidence also improves one's ability to socialise.

Increasing one's level of self-assurance is associated with an increase in overall happiness.

It has been shown that an increase in a person's level of self-confidence is closely linked to an improvement in their overall performance. For instance, when someone is beginning anything new, such as a video game or a new sport, they will naturally get better as they continue to practise it. This is because practise makes perfect. It is natural for a person to begin anything new with less confidence than they would want, especially on the first day of the endeavour. However, when they begin to grow better at it, they will naturally build greater confidence when they realise that their abilities have increased because they are aware of this fact. This example demonstrates how self-confidence may have a direct impact on a person's overall success in whatever endeavour that they do throughout their lifetime. People who begin new endeavours with greater levels of self-confidence often do better at such undertakings right from the start in comparison to those who have lower levels of self-confidence.

People who work in fields such as public speaking, business ownership, the performing arts, and sports are often aware of the significance of self-confidence. They are aware that if they do not have confidence in themselves, it may prevent them from attaining their full potential in their performance. They are also aware that if they have confidence in themselves, they will be able to quickly solve difficulties and go past any hurdles in order to continue working towards achieving their objective. When working with clients in the gym to lift weights, one strategy that coaches and personal trainers utilise that has shown to be highly successful is to manipulate their customers' mindsets in order to make them feel more confident in their abilities. For example, if the client's previous personal record for squats was 100 kilogrammes, the personal trainer will inform the client that their next set will be at 100 kilogrammes, even if the trainer has already added an additional 5 kilogrammes of weight to the barbell, bringing the total weight to 105 kilogrammes. When the customer is under the impression that they are lifting a weight that they have lifted successfully in the past, they have a higher level of confidence in their ability to raise the new weight. In the event that they are successful in squatting 105 kilogrammes, their personal trainer will inform them that they have really squatted 5 kilogrammes more than their previous personal record. However, if the personal trainer had informed the client before the squat that they would be adding an additional 5 kilogrammes, the client may have been scared since they had never done it before, and if they didn't have the confidence from the beginning, they may not have been able to lift the additional 5 kilogrammes due to their attitude. This strategy is used rather often in the field of sports, and it demonstrates to us that a positive mental attitude is far more valuable than a person's technical abilities.

How To Figure Out What It Is That Drives You

A comprehensive understanding of your people is required in order to choose what kind of timulu to provide and how to provide it. The best leaders show a genuine interest in each member of the team and devise unique ways to motivate their followers that are in line with the members' individual requirements and goals.

The ability to "influence behaviour" is essential to the process of motivating other people. The mobilisation of individuals to achieve pre-determined and strategic results is essential to the success of an organisation in achieving its goals. The success of uch, i depends on the retention of its team members and the inspiration (outworked through motivation) that they provide.

What exactly is it that drives you?

There is no such thing as a good or bad motivator; nonetheless, we must bear in mind that the purpose of providing motivation is to exert some kind of behavioural control. The shift in behaviour is being done to serve a shared goal or the end result of the organisation.

As was said previously, organisations that are not-for-profit provide an ethos, belief, or objective that is essential to the cause that they support. Motivating it people requires providing concrete proof of progress, good change, and results. This is the blood that circulates through the system.

The following is a list of important factors that serve as drivers of behaviour.

Profit or gain

One of the first kind of motivation that most of us are exposed to is receiving some kind of reward or incentive for our efforts. When we were younger, adults often used the "carrot and the stick" approach to discipline their children. If you act in a certain manner, you will get a reward. "Eat all of your vegetables, and then you'll be allowed to have dessert."

"Just go to bed right away, and if you're a good boy tomorrow, I'll buy you that toy." As an adult, the methods are exactly the same, despite the fact that the means are somewhat more sophisticated. If you reach the goal, you will be rewarded with a bonus, a salary rise, a promotion, and other perks.

The end result

One of the most important factors that drives many people is the prospect of reaching their goal. Many of you get your drive from "seeing" the end result that you've worked towards. An gratifying reward and a feeling of personal and corporate accomplishment come from seeing goals and achievements through to completion.

Seeing a project through to its conclusion is not only very fulfilling but also one of my top picks for favourite motivators. The celebration of successful completion is a reward for many people, and regardless of how that reward was earned, the influence it has on encouraging others is immense.

Positional - Influence It is a common goal of leaders to exert influence on others, and the positions they hold often provide them opportunities to do so. Even if some of the people who have had the most significant impact on history did it without holding a recognised job, the majority of us still react more to titles than we do to functions.

It is sufficient for the purposes of this chapter to acknowledge that the need to control the conduct of others is often done via the medium of position. Although there are many other ways to exert influence, this chapter will focus on the most common method. Those who see such a medium as a hierarchical power base are often motivated to progress both through and as a result of it.

Personal Development There are several purposes that may be served by training and development.

It provides organisational consistency and serves the organization's purpose.

It creates an atmosphere conducive to personal growth and serves as a recruitment base, both of which have the potential to impart corporate vision and value.

A stringent measurement for quality control and a strategic timeframe are both provided as a result of this.

It captures talent and incorporates it into the organization's future growth and development in a way that is both predictable and foreseeable.

People who have a strong desire to continue their education in a certain skill often have a strong desire to future-proof their employment and are willing to forego other motivating reasons in order to focus on their own personal development.

Being a part of

When deciding which organisations should get investments, one of the most important considerations is whether or not they are a part of something that is bigger than themselves. A sense of belonging is, without a shadow of a doubt, one of the most powerful motivators in the world of non-profit organisations.

Being able to see oneself as contributing to the larger whole while still having a role to play is a significant incentive for many people. It is not a question of whether individuals will invest their "kill" and abilities; rather, the question is where they will do so. Providing a setting in which people feel as if they belong is a far more powerful motivation than other factors.

Fear

Fear is still used to control behaviour and outcomes, despite the fact that today's society is more politically correct than ever before. Quite often, I come across the "uch method," which refers to the use of heavy techniques to increase input and maximise effort from personnel.

Fear by itself is inadequate to govern behaviour, since it is a weak motivator because it does not include the possibility of consequence. Failure to meet goals, low productivity or results, outsourcing, a slowdown in the economy, being made redundant, being fired, having one's salary cut, or being demoted are all methods that may be used to motivate people to change their conduct.

Love Coming in last, but certainly not in last place, love is a powerful force. Agápe, Éro, Philia, and Storge were the four ways in which the ancient Greeks defined the concept of love. Regardless of the method in which someone experiences love, its motivation may be expressed in powerful ways. Love encompasses not just feelings but even deeds as well. When someone "acts" with true care or love for another, it drives many different kinds of loyalty and changes in conduct.

We are more receptive to acts of love rather than words of love.

Because of this, individuals will "go the extra mile" for the family vision, as well as support, invest in, uphold, protect, and even fight for it. A compilation of all other types of motivation, loyalty is shown when one person shows loving appreciation for the efforts of another. Loyalty is a compilation of all other forms of motivation.

Be discerning. When choosing your partners, use extreme caution. You are a perfect reflection of the individuals you spend the most time with. Get rid of the negative influences that others have had on you throughout your life. Your attire, if you will. When you purchase a brand, you give out an impression of who you are. Be conscious of the people your money is going to and the causes it is supporting while making financial decisions. Your selection of groceries leaves a trace, just like every other transaction you make. Purchase food that has been grown in a sustainable manner and is beneficial to your health. Be conscious of the fact that taking in new sights and noises may invigorate your soul and motivate your ingenuity. Take note of the programmes and channels that you tune in to and watch.

Focus inward. Again, people all over the globe are eager to share their wisdom with you, and there are several paths that have been paved for you to follow in your journey through life. If you live your life intentionally and choose your own path, pay attention to what other people tell you to do, but ultimately, you need to go inside yourself to find the answers that are right for you. Get in touch with your inner voice by going within. Have faith in the voice that lives within you.

The welfare of society depends on you maintaining a firm grasp on whatever it is you now possess. In any event, there are a great many things that are deserving of being given up. It is well worth it to let go of your pessimism and judgement towards other people and the circumstances they find themselves in. You will not find success with any option. In addition, it is beneficial to cut off any connections. Let go of the need that you must remain connected to your wishes, aims, dreams, and goals. Keep working towards the goals you have set for yourself in your day-to-day life, but don't be afraid to let go along the way. You don't need to have a firm grip on anything in order to tie your sense of self-worth to your level of achievement in a certain endeavour.

Respect the present moment. You are most likely residing in a moment that has already occurred or that has not yet been conceived about. Will it locate you at this time? According to what Eckhart Tolle advises us, "Anything the present time has, embrace it as if you had opted for it." Avoid making the same errors and having the same negative experiences as before, as well as thinking about the agony over and over in your head. There is no reason to be concerned about things that have not yet occurred. Focus on the here and now. Keep your attention on the task at hand.

Demonstrations of absolution performed repeatedly and routinely. We continue to harbour sentiments of bitterness and engage in harmful behaviours, firmly grasping the coal of equity in the palms of our hands. When we stubbornly cling to our hostility and refuse to make amends for wrongs committed against us, the burning coal eventually burns our very own hands. Individuals should be forgiven and cleared of blame for the many little offences they have committed against you.

Focus on the things that you already own. If we focused more on the successes and experiences we've already had in life, rather than the ones we're still striving for, don't you think it would be more enjoyable? The more we focus on what we already possess and express gratitude for it, the less we will operate from a place of lack or desire in our daily lives. When we concentrate on what we already own, we feel more content.

Be generous with your gifts. Giving is the only situation in which it is appropriate to contribute without expecting anything in return. If you are in a position to serve, you should. There is not a strong reason to consider assisting other individuals who are in a difficult situation. When you are there to help someone else, there is very little chance that anything will go wrong. Every day, make it a point to look for more ways you may assist others.

Exercise some compassion. Develop some compassion not just for other people but also for yourself. Put an end to your perfectionist tendencies and stop setting such stringent expectations for yourself. Love should come from inside, and one should cultivate joy in order to purge oneself of pessimism. Extend your capacity for empathy to include other individuals. Instead of feeling disdain and passing judgement, strive to empathise with people and attempt to understand the circumstances in which they find themselves.

Take in the serene atmosphere. The globe may be compared to a loud market. Your brain is as well. The most effective method to restrict both your thinking and your life is to increase your rate of reflection. Find ways to stay still and make it a practise so that you may become more conscious of your own reflections. Being cautious helps one to live their life in a more considered manner. Clarity and voluntary action are both prompted by practising mindfulness. You should not worry when the television is turned off and there is no loud music playing.

Respect for Oneself

If you are able to cultivate a high sense of self-worth, you will be in a better position to tackle challenges front on. attempt out new skills even if you may not be particularly good at them at first, but be willing to accept that all you can do is attempt. I am aware that if I tried ballroom dancing for the first time, I could struggle, but that is okay. It doesn't make me a worthless person; it simply indicates I don't have much experience in that particular field. On the other side, my closest friend is someone who randomly attempted ballroom dancing and ended up being really decent at it. Because he is so upbeat about life and is always up for trying new things, he is one of the reasons why I consider him to be my best friend.

Your level of self-acceptance, the value you place on yourself, and the notion you have of yourself are the components that make up your self-esteem.

How you accept yourself in the present moment is the foundation of self-worth and self-acceptance.

This has been a challenge for me since I've always been an ambitious person, and when I'm not accomplishing enormous objectives, I'm not happy with my life.

Self-concept is more about determining how important you are to the world and what you believe you can provide to others. This has often not been a problem for me since I am an ambitious person and I like to establish objectives for myself.

However, if one's sense of self-acceptance and value is low, this will have a negative impact on other aspects of one's self-esteem as a whole.

In conclusion:

How much you respect yourself, how much you like yourself, and how you view yourself presently are all components of self-esteem. Self-acceptance and a healthy self-concept are the building blocks of healthy self-esteem.

How you feel about yourself in the present moment is how you accept and value yourself.

Your image and the value that you think you provide to the world are both components of your self idea.

Confidence may refer to how well you think you can do a certain task or face a challenge in a certain area of life; but, if you have high self esteem, you are more likely to have greater levels of general confidence when approaching tasks.

Mindset

Because this is the name of the book, it is only natural that I would want to explain what I mean by "mindset" in this work. Your mindset is how you look at life and how you see yourself in it. This therefore results in the deeds and choices that you do throughout your life. I hope that by the time you finish reading this book, you will have developed a mentality that is characterised by the highest possible levels of self-esteem and confidence.

Honor Your Own Sense Of Worth And Dignity.

It is time to celebrate your self-esteem, and the more you do so, the more optimistic your ideas will become about yourself. It is not a tough procedure to comprehend, and it is not even difficult to carry out. The difficulty is to have persistence since that is how you win at this game. persistence is the key.

Affirmations 2 is a recording by Louise Hay.

Several chapters' worth of coverage was devoted to revisiting Louise Hay and her use of positive affirmations. This point bears repeating since it is fundamental to what it means to persevere. You will notice an instant boost to your confidence after engaging in the practise of positive affirmations; nevertheless, it is imperative that you continue engaging in the practise. Your level of happiness, love, self-confidence, and fulfilment will all increase if you follow this course of action, as will your sense of self-worth.

Ensure that you speak the affirmations aloud on a regular basis and at numerous points throughout the day. "Every day, in every way possible, I am getting better and better." It is necessary for you to either consciously experience these affirmations by listening to them or subtly experiencing them when you are sleeping or meditating. Therefore, allow these affirmations to take hold inside of you. Let them develop to their full potential. Continued effort.Continued effort.Continued effort.

By Substituting One Negative Thought About Yourself With One Positive Thought About Yourself

As was shown before, ideas have a material existence. Thoughts have the power to bring forth physical manifestations. It is possible for thoughts to become manifest directly from the energy that they are composed of. The world is shaped by our thoughts. As a result of this, you have the ability to immediately boost your self-esteem by changing one of your negative self-thoughts into one of your positive self-thoughts.

Continue in this manner. You will gradually replace any negative self-thoughts with more positive ones as you continue to work on this. Affirmations allow you to take control of your future and make changes there without affecting the past. Nevertheless, the current moment is where you should focus most of your energy to improve your sense of self-worth. RIGHT NOW. Don't put it off till the next day. Begin now to rid your mind of negative ideas and replace them with good ones.

Establish Objectives

If you accomplish what you set out to do or at least put in a good faith attempt to do so, goal setting may be an effective tool for improving your sense of self-worth. Do not use the process of goal setting as another tool to berate or criticise oneself. Consider it a step in the right direction. Utilise it as a stepping stone on the path to goal success, enhanced self-esteem, and rewards.

Do not get preoccupied with the proper method of goal-setting or the proper procedure. Avoid engaging in anything that can prompt you to have unfavourable thoughts about yourself. If you allow it, anything might serve as an excuse for you to think adversely about anything. Writing down your objectives is the one and only step of the procedure that you will be required to complete. You have to put them in writing. If you don't put things in writing, you won't be able to attain them. When we say "write them down," we don't mean on a smartphone or tablet; we mean in a diary.

If the objectives you establish are not personal to you and do not really important to you, then you will lack the motivation to work towards achieving them. Create optimistic ideas about your objectives, including what they will accomplish for you and the ways in which you might enhance your life if you are successful in achieving them.

Accomplish Your Objectives and Reward Yourself

It is impossible for us to overstate how essential it is to your sense of pride and competence in yourself that you accomplish these objectives and give yourself a reward for doing so. If you are concerned about your self-esteem, it is best to avoid setting any objectives at all rather than to establish goals for yourself and then fail to achieve them. After you have accomplished them, you should give yourself a reward for your hard work. This is also quite significant. Ensure that you generate positive affirmations as part of that reward system, and make sure that you continue to remind yourself what a fantastic achievement this is.

The Synopsis and the Game Plan

- If you haven't already started one, get yourself a diary dedicated to building your self-esteem right now. Make use of that diary as the area where you chronicle your affirmations, review your objectives, and put them down in writing.

• Please respond to these questions in the most forthright manner possible. It will give you a lot of insight into how you function and will show you what kinds of affirmations and objectives you need to set for yourself.

What actions have you taken in the past that you now wish you hadn't?

What are some things that you have done in the past that you do not feel guilty about?

How often do you catch yourself saying something critical to yourself during the day?

How often do you catch yourself thinking something bad about yourself that you don't actually voice?

How often do you find yourself saying "I can't" in a single day?

Be trustworthy. Be truthful in your responses, even if they make you feel uneasy. Feel free to express whatever emotion you want in response to this, but remember to take stock of how you're affected before moving on. After you have put them down on paper, you will discover that you are more at ease with the answers as well as with yourself.

• Always have an upbeat and optimistic attitude. We have spoken about the concept of positive self-talk; nevertheless, if you really want to enhance your self-esteem, you will want to speak favourably to yourself at all times. Make your house into a fortress of happy ideas. I know this may seem corny, but it's important. Place post-it notes or posters about the home that include motivational quotes or positive affirmations. Continue making adjustments to the messages so that they do not get stale. Get rid of those who are always finding fault with everything. And try to surround yourself solely with people who have a good outlook on life, since this will help to reinforce the thinking patterns you already have.

How to Adapt an Optimistic Way of Thinking

The thing is as follows: It is quite normal for individuals to revel in the negative aspects of their lives. It's similar to how some individuals have an easier time comprehending the possibility that bad things may occur as opposed to considering the possibility that good things may and WOULD truly take place.

Consider the following: How exactly can thinking negatively benefit you in any way? Does it make your life easier or better in any way? Or does it simply make you believe that life will always be the same as it is now, and that it is impossible for it to grow any better?

It is not difficult to see how individuals may have ended up in such a state. After all, there are certain experiences in life that have the potential to shatter you or make you stronger than you were before. There are certain things in life that have the potential to completely shatter the rose-colored glasses that you have on.

However, do you know what? It's possible that it's high time for you to reawaken the kid that lives deep inside you and begin to believe in good things once again.

Begin on a Dime

Of course, it is not that simple to accomplish, particularly when you have gone through a lot in life, but you may begin by just considering the following things:

Recognise the Positive Aspects of Yourself

When you feel as if all of your bad thoughts are causing you to lose your vision, remind yourself that there are many wonderful things in your life, and you know what? That is a nice beginning to remind you that you may be appreciative for your life and that those wonderful and lovely things can happen to you as well.

Have joy in the life you have.

Take pleasure in them. Realise that there is nothing wrong with appreciating the nice things that you have because if you don't, you'll undoubtedly feel empty when the bad things come. If you don't realise this, you'll feel hollow because there is nothing wrong with appreciating the good things that you have.

Look for the Positive Aspect in Every Negative Situation.

Even though it is really challenging, you shouldn't let that deter you from giving it a go anyhow. Not at all, of course. You and your significant other may have just parted ways; if this is the case, allow yourself some time to grieve, but also keep in mind that you now have a fresh start to rediscover who you are and to re-enter the exciting world of dating. It's possible that you've lost something, but maybe this is only a means for you to make room for something even greater. Try to keep in mind that even if you may have unpleasant times in the future, this does not indicate that you will never again experience pleasant times in the future. A life that is devoid of all difficulties is not one that is really worth living.

Explore the Opportunities That Life Has to Offer

It doesn't matter who you are or what your life has been like; you always have the opportunity to improve yourself and to enjoy the best that life has to offer, regardless of who you are or what your life has been like. Do not deny oneself the opportunity to have this notion.

Keep moving forward with a positive attitude down the path that your life has set for you.

The zeal with which a person lives their life and the resilience with which they bounce back from setbacks are two qualities that set exceptional individuals apart from those who are just average.

Instead of focusing on who you have been, try to visualise who you have the potential to become in the future.

See? A lot of nice things may happen in your life right now if you only adopt the mindset that positive thinking is the best way to think. Just take a moment to consider all the wonderful things that could occur in the future.

Printed in the USA
CPSIA information can be obtained
at www.ICGtesting.com
LVHW021350051023
760085LV00064B/1997